Overground, Underground

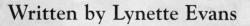

Written by Lynette Evans

Italy

My name is Adriana. I live in Italy. My country is home to the world's second-longest road tunnel, the world's wackiest leaning building, and a city with 400 bridges. Do you know why Italy has so many tunnels and bridges?

Contents

Look for the **Activity Zone!**
When you see this picture, you will find
an activity to try.

Built by People

Cities are full of structures that people have built. Roads and railroads crisscross the land. Bridges arch over rivers and valleys. Homes, schools, and stores line the streets, and tunnels twist and turn under the ground. Pipes and wires run beneath the streets, and skyscrapers, monuments, and other buildings tower high above everything else.

In countries such as Italy, some of the structures are hundreds or even thousands of years old. They stand among brand-new buildings and modern highways.

Rome is sometimes called "the Eternal City," because it has been a powerful center for thousands of years. Today, many people live and work in buildings that are hundreds of years old.

Italy has two main mountain ranges: the Apennines and the Alps. Tunnels through the Alps connect Italy to both France and Switzerland.

Steep Hills and Valleys

Italy has many steep, hilly regions. In the past, there were few roads in these places, and transportation was often difficult. People in seaside towns traveled by sea rather than road. Today, modern tunnels and bridges carry people and goods quickly and easily through the hills and over the valleys.

Materials and Forces

One of the first things any builder does is choose which materials to use. Different materials react to forces in different ways. If builders know what kinds of forces will act on a structure, it helps them choose the right materials for the job. There are five main forces that structures must cope with. Take a look at this example.

A twisting force, called *torsion* (wind pushing the top of the tower)

A pulling force, called *tension* (in the ropes holding up the bells)

A squashing force, called *compression* (the weight of the bell-tower bricks pushing down)

A *shearing*, or tearing, force (when earthquakes move or crack the ground below)

A *bending* force (the weight of people standing in the middle of floor boards)

material   something, such as wood or stone, that is used to make other things

An egg, a nest, a piece of honeycomb, and a skeleton are all natural structures. They are each made of the right material for their purpose.

Try these experiments to learn more about forces. You will need

- twigs
- modeling clay
- a piece of fabric
- safety goggles
- a rubber band
- string
- wire

Design a way to record what happens. You could use drawings, charts, or lists. Be careful! Wear safety goggles during this experiment.

1. **Compression (squashing)**
   Take a twig and push inward from each end. Is a thin twig stronger than a thicker one? Try squashing a similar-shaped piece of modeling clay.

2. **Tension (stretching)**
   Try stretching the different materials. Which ones stretch? Which resist stretching? Which ones break?

3. **Torsion (twisting)**
   Choose materials to try twisting. Notice how each material behaves.

4. **Bending**
   Take a twig and watch carefully as you bend it until it breaks. What happens to the upper surface? What happens to the lower surface?

1

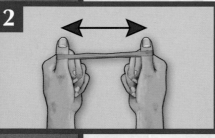

2

3

4

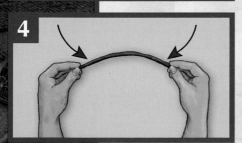

7

Empire Builders

Some structures built long ago have stood the test of time. Two thousand years ago, the city of Rome was the control center of a powerful empire, or group of countries, that stretched across parts of present-day Europe, Africa, and the Middle East.

The ancient Romans built long, straight roads to carry supplies and messengers to all parts of their empire. They also built restaurants, apartments, and grand public buildings. Some of these structures still stand, and many of the methods and materials the ancient Romans invented are still used.

Ancient Roman ruins

The ancient Romans perfected a very useful building material—concrete. They made it by mixing lime, sand, and water with rubble. Today, concrete is still made in this way.

Nowadays, engineers, planners, and architects design structures by drawing plans, called *blueprints*, and by building models. Computer programs, such as CAD (computer-aided design) programs, speed up the process.

A blueprint

architect a person who designs buildings

Roads and Races

The ancient Romans were expert road builders. They knew that a straight road made for a fast journey. They used a special measuring tool, called a *groma,* to figure out the most direct route. Over time, they constructed a network of straight, well-drained, long-lasting roads that crisscrossed the entire empire.

Today, more and more roads and freeways are being built in cities around the world. Engineers design roads for speed and safety. They build them to withstand earthquakes and heavy loads.

For safety, roads must be kept in good condition. They need to be repaired and resealed regularly.

Like modern roads, some old Roman roads sloped slightly downward at the sides. Planners call this arch the road's *camber*. It causes rain to run off the road rather than damage its surface.

Today, some world-famous road races take place in Italy. Every spring, the world's best cyclists compete in the Tour of Italy cycle race. They race down mountain roads and cross the full length of Italy in just three weeks.

Italians are also known for their love of fast cars and motor racing. Ferraris are fast, luxury Italian cars that were first made for racing.

Tracks and Trains

In almost all countries of the world, railroad tracks stretch from city to city across the land. Trains are used for moving both freight and passengers at high speeds across great distances.

Super-fast express trains have been an important part of Europe's transportation system for many years. These sleek, or streamlined, trains link countries such as Italy, France, and Germany. The world's fastest rail trains are pulled by electric engines. The electricity is supplied by cables that hang above the track.

Driver controls

Pantograph: picks up electric current from overhead lines

Traction motor: an electric motor that drives the wheels

Streamlined body

freight   goods being transported to another place

What Are Aerodynamics?

Most modern trains, planes, boats, and cars have a shape that allows air to flow easily around them. This is called an *aerodynamic* shape. A vehicle that is aerodynamic can travel at high speeds more safely because it is not being buffeted by air currents. It also uses less fuel, because it does not have to push as hard to move forward.

Maglev trains can travel faster than rail trains. Powerful magnets allow maglev trains to float just above the tracks. Computers turn electromagnets in the tracks on and off, pulling the trains forward at speeds of up to 343 mph.

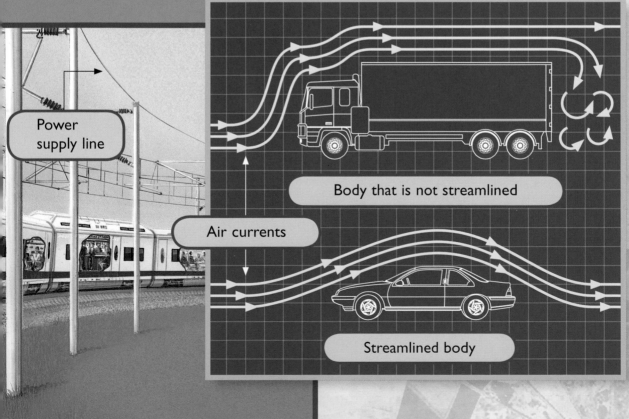

Power supply line

Air currents

Body that is not streamlined

Streamlined body

Tunnels and Tubes

Some of the oldest tunnels in the world were built in ancient Rome. Some carried water, and others formed a maze of underground cemeteries called *catacombs*.

Tunnels and subway systems in cities around the world allow people to travel quickly and easily below city traffic. In the past, the high peaks of the Alps were a barrier between Italy and central Europe. Today, the world's second-longest road tunnel runs beneath the Alps, connecting Italy and Switzerland.

The twin tunnels of the St. Gotthard Road Tunnel carry traffic for more than ten miles beneath the Alps.

Rome's roads are very busy. Rather than sit in traffic jams, thousands of workers travel on Rome's subway system, known as the Metropolitana.

Under the Sea

The world's longest underwater tunnel links Britain with the rest of Europe. When the tunnel was built, enormous boring machines were lowered into the ground, where they cut through solid rock below the sea. Now, high-speed trains take just over two hours to travel from London to Paris.

Tunnel Design Challenges

- Tunnels must be dry.
- Tunnels must not collapse.
- Tunnels need fresh air.
- Rescue workers need access.

Building Bridges

Without bridges, every stream, river, and steep valley is an obstacle to travelers. The first bridges that people made were just the trunks of fallen trees. The ancient Romans used an arch shape to build long, strong bridges. They figured out that many arches together could cross enormous distances. Most of the bridges the ancient Romans built were designed to carry water across valleys. These bridges are called *aqueducts*. Today, bridges are an important part of our transportation systems. They make journeys shorter and easier.

obstacle   something that is in the way

Bridge Basics

Water always flows to the lowest point and then stops. Ancient aqueducts helped channel water from a high source to a city on lower ground.

There are four main types of bridges: the beam bridge, the cantilever bridge, the arch bridge, and the suspension bridge.

Beam bridge—the simplest bridge; it is good for short distances only.

Cantilever bridge—this type of bridge is formed with two platforms, each one supported at one end only.

Arch bridge—the arch shape spreads the weight, providing strength.

Suspension bridge—steel cables support the weight of the platform.

The Italian city of Venice has about four hundred bridges. Venice is built on a series of islands crisscrossed by canals. The first settlers fled there hundreds of years ago to escape attackers. When they ran out of space, they made the islands larger by sinking poles deep into the muddy lagoon and building homes on stilts. Today, people get around by using boats and bridges.

At Home in Ancient Rome

Homes provide shelter, security, and privacy.
Public buildings provide places to meet, work, and
play. The ancient Romans built public shopping
plazas, stadiums, and baths. Many people could
not read or write, so instead of signing contracts,
they made business deals in public, where others
could witness them.

In about the year 217, Emperor
Caracalla had a huge public bath
built in Rome. Around it, there were
gardens, sports fields, lecture halls,
and libraries.

Rain runs
off the
overlapping
roof tiles.

Sauna

Jogging track

Thick walls keep
out summer heat.

Wooden beams
support the roof tiles.

Gymnasium

About 1,600 people could use the public baths at any one time. Water from aqueducts was heated over fires in the basement.

Dome-shaped roof and arch-shaped windows for strength

Columns support the roof.

Food shop

Bathing pool

Cool and decorative tiled floors

Changing rooms

The Test of Time

Traditional Italian homes look very similar to many built in the days of ancient Rome. Orange-tiled roofs are still an important feature of Italian towns. Thick brick or stone walls keep homes cool in the summer and warm in the winter. However, most homes now have heating, plumbing, and electricity and are filled with modern machines.

Machines at Work

Whether people are building a tall skyscraper or a deep tunnel, they use machines to make the work easier. Hand tools are simple machines. Power tools and large machines are more powerful. They get their energy from fuel rather than human muscle.

Many kinds of machines are used on a construction site to lift, move, cut, drill, and connect building materials. Cranes lift heavy materials to workers on high-rise buildings. Materials are delivered to a building site by the truckload. Concrete arrives in concrete mixers, ready to be poured.

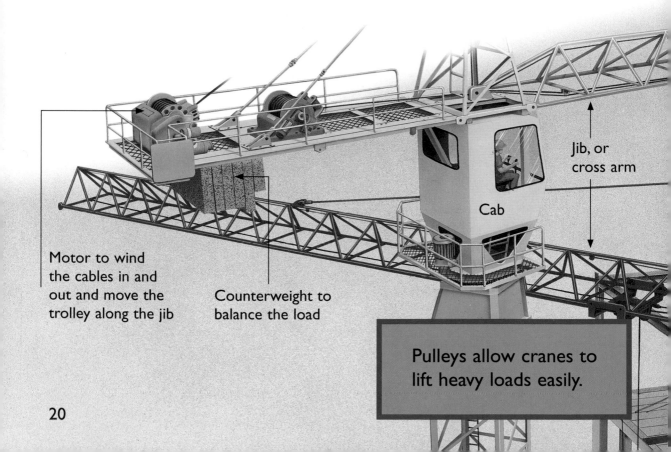

Jib, or cross arm

Cab

Motor to wind the cables in and out and move the trolley along the jib

Counterweight to balance the load

Pulleys allow cranes to lift heavy loads easily.

The drum of a concrete mixer turns constantly, preventing the concrete mixture from setting until it is poured.

Trolley

Pulley reels

Pulley cables

Lifting with Levers

A lever is a simple machine that allows heavy objects to be moved more easily. Levers usually have a long beam. Effort, or work, is applied by muscle or machine power to make the lever pivot at a point called the *fulcrum*. This causes the load, or weight, to move.

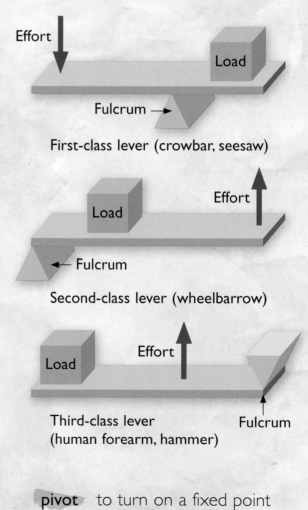

Effort

Load

Fulcrum ➙

First-class lever (crowbar, seesaw)

Effort

Load

← Fulcrum

Second-class lever (wheelbarrow)

Load

Effort

Fulcrum

Third-class lever (human forearm, hammer)

pivot to turn on a fixed point

Going Under

Just as trees are supported by their roots, buildings are supported by structures called *foundations*, which lie underground. The taller the building, the deeper its foundations need to be. The foundations keep the building from sinking, leaning, or moving.

Support systems, such as pipes and cables, run beneath many city streets. Pipes transport water and gas and take away waste. Cables carry electricity and supply telephone and television services.

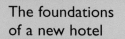

The foundations of a new hotel

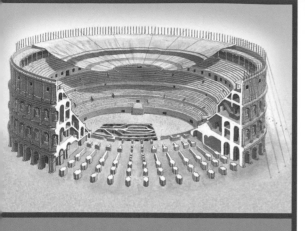

The ancient Romans built a huge theater called the *Colosseum*. They began by digging a wide, oval trench 18 feet deep. They filled the trench with concrete to form a solid foundation, which still supports the building's remains.

This famous Italian building, the Leaning Tower of Pisa, is an example of what happens when foundations give way. The tower, which was begun in 1173, started to lean almost right away. Its foundations are very shallow, and its weight caused the unstable layer of clay below to sink. Recently, the tower has been stabilized to prevent it from leaning over any farther.

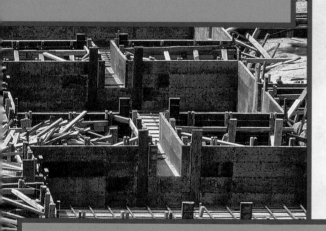

The NEC Supertower in Tokyo, Japan, has extra-wide foundations designed to ride the waves of an earthquake, protecting the building above. Its underground space is used for parking.

23

Find Out More!

Since ancient times, people have built structures that have changed the way the world looks. Find out more about one of these structures:

- the Great Wall of China
- the Suez Canal
- the Eiffel Tower
- the pyramids of Egypt
- the Hoover Dam
- the Golden Gate Bridge

To find out more about the ideas in *Overground, Underground,* do research at a library or on the Internet.

Index